With best wishes.

Colin

CW01593972

Ringing

RINGING OUT THE OLD

by

Colin Campbell

WESTBURY BOOKS

Copyright © Colin Campbell 1999
Illustrations © Gordon Redrup 1999

First published in 1999 by Westbury Books
Colin Campbell
6 Westbury Close
Fleet
Hants
GU13 9HR

The right of Colin Campbell to be identified as the author of the work has been asserted herein in accordance with the Copyright, Designs and Patents Act 1988.

All rights reserved. This book is sold subject to the condition that it shall not, by way of trade or otherwise, be lent, resold, hired out or otherwise circulated without the publisher's prior consent in any form of binding or cover other than that in which it is published and without a similar condition including this condition being imposed on the subsequent purchaser.

ISBN 0-9531668-2-1

Typeset by Amolibros, Watchet, Somerset
This book production has been managed by Amolibros
Printed and bound by Professional Book Supplies, Oxford, England

Contents

Harold II, 1022-1066

Last in the line of Saxon kings,
you defeated Hardrada's Norwegians
at Stamford Bridge.
But William's legions
I've heard say
won the day
on the occasion
of that Norman invasion.

Having quelled the natives' uprising,
the Conqueror started colonising.

Song Of The Domesday Book, 1086

Verse

William is putting a national tax on
Virgates and hides of each subjected Saxon.
Householders filling the Conqueror's coffers,
Unsure what this form of registry offers.
Sincerely we hope it will be complimentary
To praiseworthy citizens, peasants and gentry.

Chorus

But beware! It's the first compilation for ages
Set by commissioners on sheepskin pages.
Some say it's the advent of Administration—
A Norman idea of controlling the nation.
So, look to the future, forgetting times past,
This idea of taxing we don't think will last...
This idea of taxing we don't think will last.

Death of William Rufus, 1100

Accident or assassination?

A segment of history
clad in mystery
about the arrow from Tyrell's bow.
Will we ever know
the truth, to blame or condone
one that brought death? A forest stone
bears mute remembrance.

Thomas Becket, December 29th 1170

Slain by knights from second Henry's court
that sought
the end of priestly turbulence,
close to the first martyr's day.

Enthroned, you held sway
over Canterbury's see
before years of royal remorse
and penitence.

Simon de Montfort, 1208-1265

I, the Earl of Leicester
defeated the third Henry,
being victorious at Lewes.

A song was sung
among
those who supported me
with baronial fidelity.

Yes, Lewes was a victory—
but at Evesham my obituary
was read
after the short parliament.

Magna Carta, 1215

At Runnymede
not far from the Staines by-pass,
John set his seal
on a document concerning every class
of citizen.
A sort of New Deal
for the rights of men,
from pauper to prince.
Put down on parchment then
and adhered to ever since.

Geoffrey Chaucer, 1340-1400

Of course a
paean to Chaucer
never fails
to record *Canterbury Tales*,
written at his height,
mentioning that "parfit gentil knight"—
although, as academics tell,
he did write other things as well.

Wat Tyler and the Peasant Revolt, 1381

It was subordination that caused resentment,
the unprecedented commencement
of uprising.
There had even been guidelines on who could wear fur.
Strangely, it never seemed to occur
to yeomen minds
that the divisions in our English social life
could lead to unrest and further strife
in the country.
The people rallied under their hero from Kent,
and in rebellious mood they went
towards London where they publicly expressed misgivings and fears;
the revolt lasting only three years—
their leader dead.

William Caxton, 1422-1499

Bringing to the barren page
your fifteenth century blueprint
for a future age.
The living word set down
to delight,
to stimulate learning
and satiate yearning
from your binding
of boundless knowledge.

The Wars of the Roses, 1455-1485

Beginning at St Albans
two roses battled
after half-time of a century,
until the final round
on unsporting Bosworth Field.
Here Richard was killed
before a princess and Henry
were united in love.
Thirty years of parochial war
yielding to the Rose of Tudor.

William Byrd, 1542-1623

He played the organ
above Lincoln's aisles—
a lofty position.

Skilful in composition
for voices, keyboard, viols.

England's Palestrina;
pastoral poet of the age.
Fine craftsmanship on every page.

Has there ever been
a composer with so catholic a view?
There have, I think, been very few.

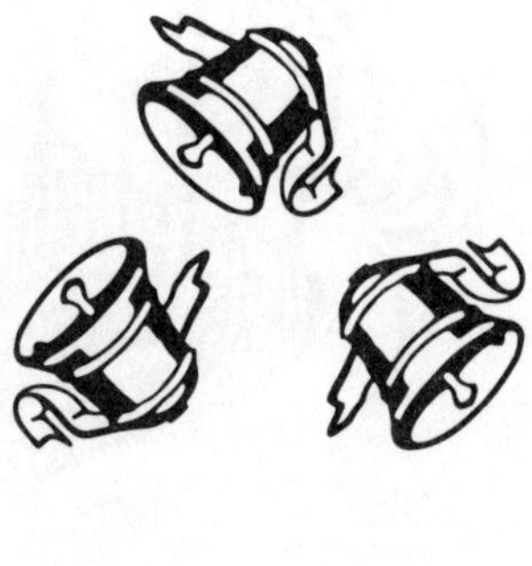

William Shakespeare, 1564-1616

I see a wall of Portia's home,
dark stones of Elsinore.
A wood near Athens.
Hear of stratagems on streets of Rome
where the Ides are said to be
feared by those in forum rule.
Watch Caliban and Prospero;
note Prince's lone soliloquy.
Scenes before Harfleur or forest glades.
The cadence of a sonnet's charm.
A man for all the seasoned year
whose Dream of summer never fades.

Oliver Cromwell, 1599-1658

A Commoner, he stands at Westminster,
this man from Huntingdon who protected
us after internal war.
Serving under Essex, he rose in rank and stature,
reorganising parliamentary corps.
Victorious at Naseby, Marston Moor.
Brought about the monarch's trial,
and in his steady rise advanced kingly demise.
Our solitary martial leader—
no longer do we heed
a call for military rule;
maintaining an aversion
to coercion.

The Pilgrim Fathers

6th September, 1620

Intrepid haven seekers
sailing this September day.
By nature puritanical,
escaping satanical persecution.
Human flotsam drifting
to a distant West.
Crossing an ocean to where new-found peace
and new life
await your settlement.

Sir Christopher Wren, 1632-1723

After the Fire he planned to build
the City, projected, not fulfilled,
yet from its ashes there came
glowing embers of his fame.
St Stephen's, Walbrook, Mary-le-Bow,
and other buildings that we know.
And note the stone-carved eulogy
his "monument you wish to see".
We look about and praise such men
as this architect called Wren.

John Macadam, 1756-1836

When surfaces of highways wear
we start immortalising
the name that's linked to each repair,
and called macadamising.

Robert Burns 1759-1756

Lines on Doon's banks
rise as song to fill the mind, the heart.
In literature's pages
printed through the ages
we find
vernacular verse
of this cotter's son.
A native voice from the bothy
recites poems of Kilmarnock,
and tells of Tam O' Shanter;
as Caledonian as the pipe's skirl.

On Reading Wordsworth (1770-1850)

I've never seen a lonely cloud,
there's always been others around
swallowing planes' ascent
from distant runways.

I've watched feathery clouds
soft-broom the sky;
at a summer evening's dusk
polish and dust stars...
Clouds sweeping towards that purple shade
at the edge of the world—
but I like daffodils.

Jane Austen, 1775-1817

Jane of Overton
who writes of the Bennets
and their prejudices.
Wanders with us through Mansfield Park,
and talks with sense
and sensibility in this environment
of a fin de siècle...
Inviting us to turn pages
with her gentle persuasion.

Sir Henry Stanley, 1841-1904

Presumption

I fought with the Confederates
before joining a newspaper in New York.
Later there was talk
of a countryman in the lurch.
With a commission to search for him,
Africa bound,
I found him one November,
and put the question,
"Doctor Livingstone...?"

Richard D'Oyle Carte, 1844-1901

In days managerial
I was offered material
by William and Arthur I couldn't ignore.
At a London theatre
there was nothing better
than *Patience* and *Yeomen* and then *Ruddigore*.

Now, Gilbert was lyrical
and often satirical;
Sullivan writing in strict measured time.
With infectious bravado they spawned *The Mikado*,
a musical score closely wedded to rhyme.

Some people were critical
of the political
references penned by this pair at their height.
But, perhaps *Trial By Jury*
abated the fury,
creating an ambience made to delight.

The Great Exhibition, 1851

See the Empire pass
under Caxton's glass.
Devonshire's gardener
crystallising industry.
Joseph extolled
for his bold
enterprise,
wherein lies
a nation's achievement,
before the bereavement
of consort's Victoria.

Proud exhibitors demonstrate
to thousands massing, en fête,
Dominions' greatness...
While Wellington talks
of sparrow hawks.

Sir Arthur Conan Doyle, 1859-1930

Creator of a sleuth of crime
who fought to outwit and defeat
thugs from rooms in Baker Street.
Your stories set in olden time
of hansom cab and gaslight jet.
Your Mister Holmes his violin played
while furtively a trap was laid
to catch a culprit in a net
of smart detection at its best.
Although it is polite to tell
of Doctor Watson's help as well
before the time of close arrest.
Watson was the perfect foil
to Sherlock, and surprised him when
his wisdom flowed as from the pen
of you, Sir Arthur Conan Doyle.

Ralph Vaughan Williams, 1872-1958

You wrote of earth's beauty
in tranquil moving fourths for fan-vaulted choirs.
Your cutting ploughshare dissonance
tilled from folklore.

You left in an Indian summer,
with the sun ascending as the lark
to whispered strings.

A Picture by L S Lowry, 1887-1976

I see thin people in streets echoing to clogs
beside buildings' flat facades.
I count the stick people
with emaciated bodies,
legatees of a past revolution.

When did he cotton on to this idea
of using the mill as a backcloth?

Men and women immobile
yet moving to the senses.
Catching the eye in his representation
of industrial bleakness.

Bernard Law Montgomery, 1887-1976

On Africa's sand you changed the shape of war.
Your two-badged beret a symbol of defiance.
At times driving colleagues to their limit
while you drove enemies to retreat
past wadis of the Sahara,
sealing victory.

T E Lawrence, 1888-1935

An enigma of deserts...
Many have tried to wipe the dust
from searching eyes looking for truth.
They find contradictions
in their burrowing
like an archaeological dig.
You engaged in Arab revolt,
and blotted out post-war
identification with a martial alias
or two.
To some, a superhero
spurring dangers in hostile lands,
then to die on a Dorset road.
A puzzling death—
an enigma.

Emily Wilding Davison, 4th June 1913

You shunned caution,
throwing yourself
in front of the hooves of Anmer.
Who can forget
the suffragette
at Epsom Downs that day?
A presage
of sacrificial lives
before a world at war.
Not for you the sound of guns—
you were in Morpeth ground.

The Great War, 1914-1918

(Goodbye Piccadilly)

We didn't want to be heroes,
charging from trench into Hell
of shell burst and obliteration.
The hill to be taken;
lives measured by a few yards.
Up guards, and at 'em!—
a fatuous command bringing carnage
defying imagination.

Hesitation to fight brought shame
and the white feather,
whether idiot or scholar.
We died for the hollow glory
of those who sent us over the top
to stop a rival advance.

No man's land a sick joke,
where, under the cloak of death
our bodies surrendered to a bloody fate,
to create the sombre one-liner,
missing, presumed dead.

You remember us with poppies blood red,
we, who bled, and lie white-crossed in rows,
lost and buried under the scrap heap of war.
If you wish to pray for us,
on the eleventh day for us,
go easy on the heroics—
we didn't want to be heroes.

Musical Revolution, the 1920s

The sharp edge of Twenties' discord
was blunted by repetition.
Change of taste sweetening its acerbity.
Discarded tonality became supplanted
by novel sounds with their splash
of fierce colour.
Dazzling hues of woodwind and brass
painted on elaborate scores
accompanied advancing Depression's
ragtime syncopation.
A postlude to Flanders' carnage
when avant garde declared war
on the Romantic ear.

Early School

It all seems vague now
but I remember her pointing at the red bits
on the wall map
and saying they belonged to us.
"Did we buy them, Miss? Or were they presents?"
I couldn't understand why we sang about Jerusalem
on Empire Day. It didn't belong to us, did it?
We waved paper flags.

I heard her talk about things called Bolsheviks
that lived a long way away, further than Margate,
and carried bombs.
I heard two teachers arguing over a raincoat
called a ramsay mac, and a strange animal
called a reichstag.

They said the balloon was going up,
but I couldn't see it from the playground.
Then there was the jubilee.
We waved paper flags.
She pointed at the red bits again
and we sang some more.

Contours

In first school she produced a map.
See, she said, how lines wrap
themselves about hills.

Cramped lines mean high tors. She went
on about the deep descent—
you must take care...

Later we made the climb;
a fruitless search, a waste of time.
No lines found
upon the ground.

Great Aunt, 1932

She Sankey and Moodyed on Sundays;
mid-week when in the mood.
She talked of the old queen.

The front room rarely used.
She perused
John Bull and Titbits.

In this haven of Victoriana
I expected a prince consort to enter.
Number Eleven was the centre
for important meetings.

Dressed in black,
singing snatches from Savoy operas
and talking of early days.
Of Gilbert drowned before the war
when George was crowned.

Anything new was "fangled"—
the radio a wireless.

A tireless do-gooder.
A walking memoir
of hansom cab years.

Years Ago, the 1930s

The tick-over of a Bentley,
railway engines' horizontal smoke,
brakes shrill in sidings.

Taste of sherbet dabs before lollipops.

Thud of leather on the yard wall
kicked by Stan's Stoke City disciples.
Air swish around Ferris Wheel
felt by fairground astronauts.

Smell of heather and long grass—
more prosaic faggots and peas;
promenade fish and chips,
Summer snap of picnic celery.

A summoning bell to lessons
in high-windowed classroom.

I hear the chatter of departed friends.
Thoughts ticking over like the Bentley.

Aldershot Searchlight Tattoo, 1935

We walked in dusty school crocodile
for well over a mile
to the tattoo before the war.

No searchlights. A matinee for us.
Squashed cake, lemonade and teachers' fuss
at the tattoo before the war.

The guns of Trafalgar; skirted floats as ships,
relayed noise of cannon. Fish and chips
went with the tattoo before the war.

Sharp rifle crack, machine gun's rattle,
Light Brigade in Crimea battle
in the tattoo before the war.

Simulated death to beat of drum
presaged what we knew would come
after the tattoo before the war.

When at last appeasement died
some of us were shocked, and cried
when we heard tell how "Sir"
fell in that war after the tattoo.

George, 1936

I remember him at school.
Gullible,
Easy to coax,
Victim of a hoax
each term.

Coarse schoolboy jeers
brought him close to tears.
The easiest lad to sway
anyday.
His injured pride
Taken for a ride.

He surprised us
In the tug-of-war.
All set to win,
He dug his heels in.

An Early Catch, 1939

Superfluous light of stars
above lamp's sodium beam
wherein I run as in a dream.
A beer can clatters near bar's entrance.
There's the milk float's dawn hum;
blinded eyes—
those windows where the baby cries
invariably come in early hours.
Gurgle of drain outside The Rose and Crown.
in sporadic pools of winter rain
along the pathway
The up-train, punctual to a fault,
glides glow-worm-like to halt
to start my working day.

3rd September 1939

On this day Peace died; belfries became muted,
replaced by the glissando of a siren
bewailing our fate.
Brutality was legalised;
lives fragmented by the shrapnel of hatred,
and Love was shot through the heart.

On Guard, Chatham Barracks, 1944

They arrive late from town
taunting world's sobriety;
eyes watered by jokes.
Slurred responses to my challenge
at their slalom approach.

An absurd ritual—
I know "Who goes there"
at the main gate.

Guardians, 1944

I looked back towards them at my exit.
They stood sternly aloof
bidding me a hazy farewell
below the castle.

Years later I returned in sunshine,
bronzed.
Meeting again those sentinels,
no longer aloof but welcoming—
those pale-faced Dover cliffs.

Big Freeze, 1947

Winter's raw fist raps on autumn's door,
sketching pictures on panes.
Chilling omens of season's end
before a warming equinox.

Icicles festooning gable and gutter,
hanging around until the thaw
of dripping surrender.

A hard surface to the pond
grips stalagmite reeds
held petrified.
Ducks mystified at loss of water.

Professor, 1948

He walked with the question mark of a stoop,
pausing comma-like for breath.
Talked softly as if in parenthesis.
When he stressed a point
I felt the italics of words,
punctuating theory with humour.
No complex sentences.

Interjections were not part of speech;
his remarks suggesting lower case lettering,
the passive voice.
Originality of thought shunned
jargon, slang, the "in" word.

His death was a full stop.

Lecture Days 1950

He spoke about railways;
mentioned Mussolini ensuring
train punctuality.
The second speaker rambled on
for an hour explaining
North Sea oil rigs.
Boring.
The third tackled building societies
and, at least
produced some interest.

On The Beach, 1950

They built castles with turrets, barbicans
that crumbled under pressure
and sandy sieges.
Tides provided a momentary moat
before their defences were breached,
the battle over before tea.
Father spoke quietly of things called
landing parties; gazed towards the south
murmuring an odd mixture of names—
Sword, Juno, Gold, Omaha and Utah.
He never joined in their war games,
but sat, deck-chaired, watching them,
remembering something they didn't
understand.

Dylan Thomas, 1954

(A Play For Voices)

Early in Nineteen Fifty Four
Through the portal of a door
We walked
Into a new world...

Characters talked
in a language of magical words.

Overcome,
Struck dumb,
Enchanted we stood
Under Milk Wood.

Luton Airport, 1960

I'm an earthbound creature.
Pegasus without wings.

I've this niggling phobia about flying,
although trying
to overcome it by standing
on a high-rise landing
or sitting in ski chair lifts.
Awaiting the feel of coming
quickly
back
to
earth.

Disc Jockey, 1963

Through psychedelic haze
your tape spawns Lurv
and Howlmiss yew—
the disingenuous phrase
of a new single issue,
bestowing amid discoing
another nostrum
from your rostrum.

A Room in Majorca, 1969

The guide points to Chopin's piano,
a Broadwood from London.

An oft-repeated monologue follows.

I seem to hear an étude's cascading notes;
arpeggios sprayed as blossoms,
scenting the room.
The rhythm of a thick-chorded polonaise rnilitaire;
lilt of waltz and mazurka.

A mirage of tubercular Frederic
at the keyboard in revolutionary mood,
or producing the delicacy of a new nocturne
ready to enthral habitués of a Parisian salon.

Unemployment, 1972

The pit wheel has stopped,
rusting above slag heap and cottage.
The shaft is closed
where once black diamonds
brought community warmth,
industrial wealth.

The still air bereft of miners' song,
chatter and joke in the "snug".
No echo of band's brass
from blaring gala days.

Winter and hearts are bitter.
The pit wheel of misfortune stands
as a memorial to the closure
of mine and erosion of hope.

Thespian Art of John Gielgud, 1978

He weaves words as tapestry.
At times "sotto voce", a whisper
heard by those in the "gods".
No movement distracts them from each stressed syllable,
inflection, spaced pause,
offered for their delectation.
An alchemist capable of changing
mundane script
into embroidered language.
Enchanting the ear;
echoing until memory's final recall.

Country Walk, 1978

We go in search of peace along the lane
at weekends if the weather should be fine,
and climb a fence or step across a stile
towards the coppice holding birch and pine.
Forgetting city mayhem for a while
with all its lure of stock exchanging gain.

We walk the rise towards the wooded hill,
through bracken with a foot-worn track ahead,
and traverse rivulets, pass under trees.
The sponge-earth giving slightly at our tread,
spare branches swaying gently in a breeze.
The village far below serene and still.

From on the height we scan the spreading plain,
to distant lowlands stretching to the sea
that joins the sky in panoramic view,
united in their coloured harmony.
We turn, remembering each autumn hue,
and walk in new-found peace back to the lane.

Don't Point The Finger, 1980s

Behind the T-shirt and the jeans
what do I see?
An unsure raver in your teens,
scarcely out of puberty.

Behind bravado and your smirk
what could you be?
An adolescent out of work
mouldering in lethargy.

Behind the ghastly hell of drugs,
crass infamy.
Among some anti-social thugs
lurks a replica of me.

I think I know what this life means
to someone in T-shirt and jeans.

Arundel, 1986

Its castle a climbing greyness above the Arun,
dwarfing St Nicholas and gated town hall.
Parsons Hill and King Street ascend to cosset
the cathedral church upon its height.
Shops cling to the hill that plunges to river's bridge
and railway beyond.
Close to priory and Norfolk's keep,
playhouse boards are trod on London Road.

Streets meander like tourists who study
antiquarian books, souvenirs, windowed menus,
before dusk of a Sussex stillness envelops
reader and diner in the ancient town.

Promenade Concert, 1985

Inner cladding stifles the echo,
stopping one chord's trespass on another.
Promenaders erupt with ovations
at grand finale or poignant postlude.
Classic and avant garde with diverse sounds
enthral
in Albert's hall...
Although this première
receives the reserved judgement
of a second opinion
or more
in Kensington Gore.

After The Protest (Newbury Bypass, 1990s)

At first trees were lashed, toppled and sawn—
wooden skyscrapers thudding to earth.
Then a vista unseen for centuries
appeared through the widening gap.

The hill's brow frowned;
solitude shattered
by this annoying impertinence.
Rural life uprooted by callous machinery
as animals scampered away from invasion.

Verdant land scored, scarred
by tracks of clinging mud,
squashing to death Nature's ancient beauty.
Yielding to motorway madness
of the modern age.

Modern Miss, 1990

She's with it,
using the "in" phrase;
taking up the latest craze.
Gives you a bell when phoning.
Wears post-Carnaby dress.
Memorises pop charts;
tells you who's at Number One
this week.
Haunts discos and wine bars.
Likes fast cars.
"No way" her constant cliché.
Knows about websites
and the net.
She surmises and realises
in fifty years' time
she'll be old-fashioned—
not with it.

All of a Spin, 1992

Being a bungling possessor
of a word processor,
and aware of phobic fears,
I realise
to my surprise
old spiders netting flies
have known about web sites for years.

Depressing Deadlines, 1993

I could fill a mortuary with poems
that have died with inspiration,
raising no elation
in readers.
Of little interest then and now,
except to a pathologist's mind
perhaps hoping to find
something worthy of probing thought.

The advent of writers' block
produced that paralysis
when no critical analysis
was required of lifeless verse.
None of this post-moribund selection
could withstand resurrection.

So I'll let sleeping lines lie
and forget exhumation.

Helicopter (Air Show)

From Odiham you lift to the sky
over Hampshire countryside.
Your blades' chatter
disturbs the gliding peace of Lasham,
nearby Alton.

Over watercressed Alresford
your under-belly mirrored
in de Lucy's reservoir
once concerned with navigation.

Eastward perhaps, hop-picking ghosts
shield eyes against the sun
on county's edge,
as you manoeuvre above field and canal
in aerial spaciousness.

The Long Haul, 1994

(Charity Marathon)

It was good to know
there was just three miles to go
wearing vest and shorts.
His thoughts
were on completing
the course, not beating
any record.
Even if he came last
it wouldn't cast
doubts on his fitness would it?
Provided his feet
kept pounding the city street
in the long run
a marathon could be fun.

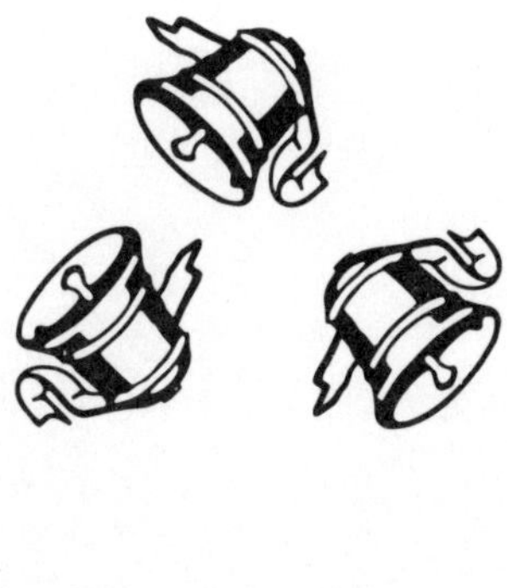

TV Intermission, 1995

Insurance company solves crisis.
River scenes along the Isis
Lure us to a new shampoo.
The AA man knows what to do.
Wonders told of washing powder,
Drivers speed like Nicki Lauda.
Cows perform a "hoofers" dance,
Ferries plough their way to France.
Monkey slurps a special tea,
Furniture is payment-free
Until April of next year—
Penguins have a taste for beer.
Strong detergents septic proof,
Spy brings chocolates from the roof.

If plots from current "soaps" seem bare,
in natural breaks all drama's there.

Hackneyed Phrases, 1995

Are we ensnared in a world of the cliché?
We paint the town red while we're having a ball.
Refusing an offer our answer is "No way!"—
A final decision is once and for all.

Any assumption is taken for granted.
A horse that's a "cert" is usually dead.
Common or garden normality's planted
After sharp differences come to a head.

The cheerful "No problem!" means there is no worry.
"You're kidding" infers you are telling a lie.
Making a dash equates with a hurry-
A time in the future becomes by and by.

A word in your ear is a way of confiding
About an old friend who was once in his prime;
An illustrious career, I am told, is subsiding.
Between you and me at this moment in time.

Someone's commanding that I have a nice day,
But lacking in money, I haven't a bean.
A slap on the back brings another old cliché—
"Well, there yer go then!"—know what I mean?

Jumble Sale, 1997

Look at them!
At two p.m.
besieging the hall,
invading each stall.
Selecting
or rejecting
hats, aprons, shoes.
Checking for size.
Some are thieving magpies
poised to attack—
vultures picking the bones
of bric-a-brac.

The Dome's Day Look, 1999

To the East of our capital, close by the Thames
See the rise of a modem rotunda!
Some place it among architectural gems,
And call it a constructed wonder.

Perhaps not a classic of oncoming years
To equal the treasures of Rome.
But still, there are those that give three hearty cheers
For this mighty Millennium Dome.

Let's hope there will soar from this riverside site
A structure that courts admiration,
To fill future Britons with fervent delight
While building up pride in their nation.

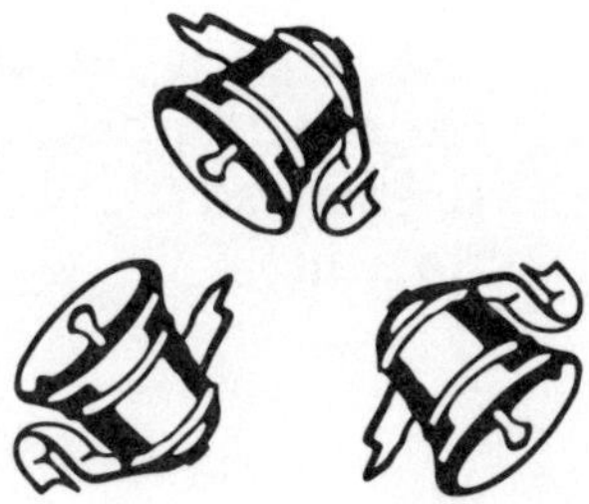

By the same author:

Farrago

There has always been a fascination for the sea and its historic coastline around Britain. Several poems in this anthology reflect this interest with a nostalgic look at childhood trips to the South Coast and memories of watching the Cunard liners negotiating the entrance to The Solent.

Those days provided a strange amalgam of the serious and the comic; the elation at the first sighting of Chichester Harbour (*Thoughts on...*) from the heights of Goodwood; perhaps the first stirrings of a love of poetry on being told that Tennyson once lived at the house called Farringford on the south side of the Isle of Wight (*Hengistbury Head* and *Coasting*); the other side of the holiday trips - candy floss, Punch and Judy, amusement arcades (*Hall of Mirrors*). All frivolities and excursions were overshadowed by the threat of war; the slender hope of appeasement ("...before mulberries became harbours"). This emphasis on nostalgia is seen in *Winter Resort* where "Old men...hear shouts of sunburnt ghosts. See visions of children...barefoot on promenade"; the more sedate holiday by the bowling green (*Summer at Worthing*).

A lifetime of music in the amateur and professional theatre and the concert platform is also recalled. There is a passing reference to a love of architecture in such poems as *Gargoyle* and *A Folly*. Advancements in the world of transport have not been overlooked - from the discarded tyre in the village pond (*Discarded Tyre*) and modern day aerobatics (*The Red Arrows*). The on-going construction of motorways is mentioned in I*nterring History*.

"As a poet he shows great understanding and technique, with excellent imagery and construction ... beautifully printed and presented ... well worth the money." Salopian Poetry Society on *Farrago*.

Price £6.95

ISBN 0-9531668-0-5, Westbury Books

Chuckleverse

Why do some people cry
Over *Madam Butterfly*?
Isn't it an opera
About lepidoptera?

As the title suggests, this is a book of quiet humour providing the reader, it is anticipated, with the occasional giggle or chuckle and a gentle appreciation of the ridiculous. Comedy can be found in the strangest and most serious of situations, serving as a palliative in stressful circumstances, and making us feel the better for its discovery. It is shown here in several forms: the play on words at The Ark's construction (*Arkwright*), the woman at the sale (*Auction*), and the New Year resolution (*Hope*). Even moments of aggravation or near disaster can be thought of with hindsight as having an underlying comical content: the telephonic salesperson (*Nuisance Call*), the errant toupee (*Topless*) or pain on the dance floor (*Lover's Plea*). Humour has survived since Genesis, and, luckily for us, shows no sign of expiring.

Price £6.95

ISBN 0-9531668-1-3, Westbury Books
Fleet
Hants
GU13 9HR